DUDLEY SCHOOLS LIBRARY
AND INFORMATION SERVICE

KU-453-222

Schools Library and Information Services

S00000658244

Material Matters
Plastics

Terry Jennings

Chrysalis Children's Books

First published in the UK in 2003 by
Chrysalis Children's Books
64 Brewery Road
London N7 9NT

© Chrysalis Books Plc 2003

Text by Terry Jennings

DUDLEY PUBLIC LIBRARIES

L   4744 3

658244   SCH
            J668.4

All rights reserved. No part of this book may be reproduced or utilized in any form
or by any means, electronic or mechanical, including photocopying, recording or by
any information storage and retrieval system, except by a reviewer, who may quote
brief passages in a review.

ISBN 1-84138-820-3

British Library Cataloguing in Publication Data
for this book is available from the British Library.

A Belitha Book

Editorial Manager: Joyce Bentley
Series Editor: Sarah Nunn
Design: Stonecastle Graphics Ltd
Picture Researcher: Paul Turner

Printed in China

10 9 8 7 6 5 4 3 2 1

Picture credits:
Roddy Paine Photographic Studios: pages 8 (left), 10, 12-13, 14-15, 16 (below), 17 (top), 19, 20-21, 23,
24, 25 (below), 28-29.
Spectrum Colour Library: pages 6-7.
Stonecastle Graphics: pages 5, 26.
Transco: page 18.

contents

plastics everywhere

You can see **plastics** almost everywhere. There are plastics in your home and at school.

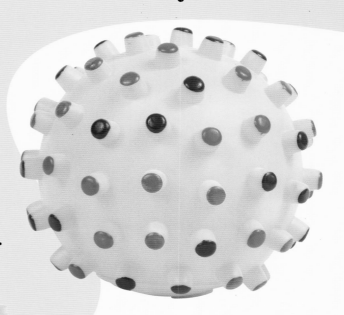

The plastic called Teflon is very slippery. It is used to coat the surface of frying pans so that the food does not stick.

Plastics are often used instead of metals, wood and glass. Plastics are light and they do not **rust** or **rot**. You can see through some plastics, while many are difficult to break. Some plastics are hard and stiff, others are soft and bendy.

You probably have toys and games made from plastic.

How are plastics made?

Plastics are **manufactured materials**. They are made in a factory. The first plastics were made from wood. Some plastics are still made from wood or coal. But most are made from **chemicals** that come from oil. Plastics are not coloured at first, so a **dye** is added to colour them.

This factory makes plastics.

These new plastic bottles will soon be ready to leave the factory.

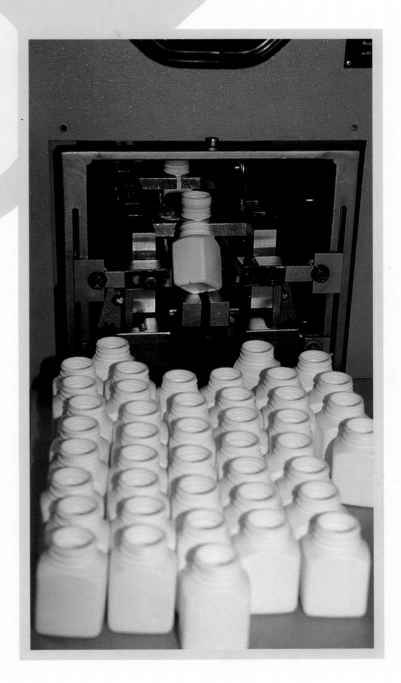

The first plastics were made over 150 years ago. They caught fire easily and so were not used very much.

7

The main kinds of plastic

There are two main groups of plastics. Some, such as those used to make telephones and radios, can only be heated and shaped once. They cannot then be made into new shapes.

These plastics can be heated and shaped only once.

These plastics can be melted and shaped many times.

The first plastic to be used a lot was called Bakelite. Early in the 20th century it was used to make radios and telephones.

Some other plastics, such as **polythene** or **polystyrene**, can be **melted** again and again. They can be made into a new shape each time.

shaping plastics

Plastics leave the factory as small white pellets. These are then melted and shaped to form bags or bottles. Some are rolled flat to make floor tiles.

This is what most plastics look like when they leave the factory.

Buckets, bowls and boxes are usually shaped by squirting the plastic into a shape, called a **mould**.

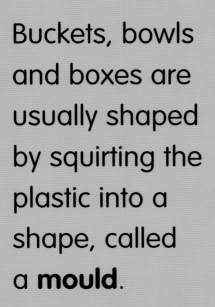

Polythene, a common plastic, was first made in the 1930s.

Even large plastic objects, like this bin, can be made using a mould.

11

Plastic toys

Many plastic toys are made in moulds. If toy bricks are being made, the mould is the shape of the brick.

The world's tallest structure made from toy bricks was built in Taiwan. It was a pyramid more than 25 metres high.

Toy bricks like these are made in a mould.

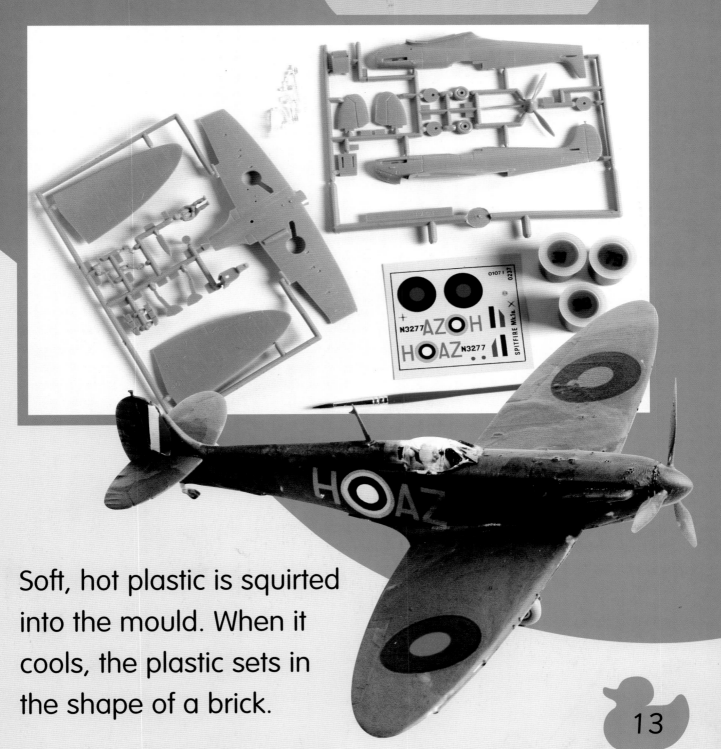

The parts of this plastic model aircraft were made in a mould.

Soft, hot plastic is squirted into the mould. When it cools, the plastic sets in the shape of a brick.

plastics for building

Many doors, window frames and pipes are made from plastic. Plastic is used because it does not rust or rot, and does not have to be painted.

Plastic doors and windows are easy to keep clean and last for a long time.

The pipes that take rainwater from the roofs of buildings are now made of plastic. They used to be made of iron.

The roofs of many **conservatories** are made of plastic. This is because the plastic material is light and you can see through it. It will not break like glass might.

plastics and electricity

Plastic is used to cover electrical wires, plugs and sockets. Electricity cannot pass through most plastics, so plastics help to keep us safe.

The plastic covering on this wire and these fuses stops electricity reaching us.

16

NEVER touch electric sockets, plugs or wires.

Many things that use electricity have a plastic covering.

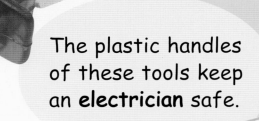

The plastic handles of these tools keep an **electrician** safe.

17

Plastic pipes

Plastic is now used for many pipes instead of metals such as iron, **lead** or **copper**.

Plastic pipes, like this gas pipe, are strong, light and bend easily.

The large pipes that carry water and gas under the streets are made of plastic. Some of the water pipes inside our homes are also made of plastic.

Plastic water pipes come in many different shapes and sizes.

plastics and our food

Some plastics help to keep our food fresh for longer. Polythene bags stop bread from drying out. Polystyrene boxes are used to keep burgers hot.

Polystyrene keeps food and drinks warm and stops us from burning our fingers.

The sides of a refrigerator also contain polystyrene. This helps to keep heat out of the refrigerator, so that our food stays cool.

Polystyrene can be made into a very light foam. It is used to pack around fragile equipment.

The plastic inside a refrigerator is easy to clean. It also helps to keep our food cool.

Plastic clothes

Some plastics can be made into fine **fibres**. These fibres are stronger than wool or cotton. If they are woven into cloth, the cloth is often **waterproof** and warm.

This girl's winter clothes are made of plastic materials. They keep her warm and dry.

22

Plastic boots are waterproof.

Sometimes plastic fibres are mixed with wool or cotton to make clothes. The plastic fibres make the clothes lighter and stronger.

Nylon, polyester and acrylic are three different types of plastic used to make fibres.

plastics keep us safe

Some plastics are very strong and light. They are used to keep us safe. The **helmets** worn by cyclists and motor cyclists are made of a strong plastic that is not heavy to wear.

This helmet is made of plastic. It **protects** the cyclist's head in an accident.

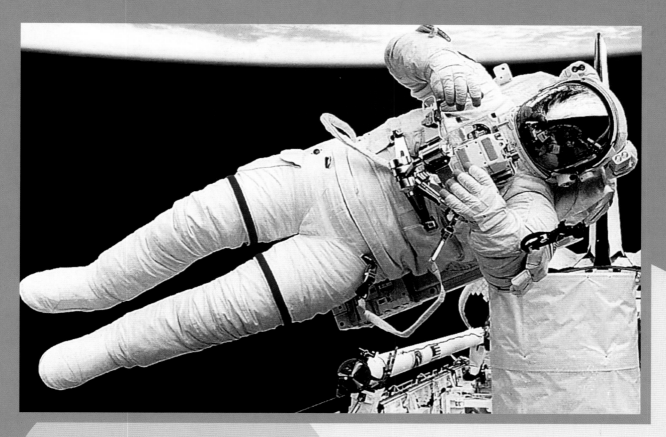

Space suits contain eight or nine layers of plastic materials. They protect the wearer from heat and cold.

Plastic sunglasses protect our eyes from the Sun's harmful rays.

25

Getting rid of waste plastic

Most plastics will not rot away. They will last for hundreds of years. Scientists are trying to make new plastic bags and wrappers that will rot away in time.

Plastic litter often gets washed up on the sea shore and has to be cleared up.

The easiest plastics to **recycle** are those that can be heated and made into new shapes.

Most plastics are made from oil. There is however only so much oil in the world, and we must use oil and plastics carefully. It is possible to reuse some kinds of plastic. This is called recycling.

These plastic bottles will be recycled and used to make fleece jackets.

Do it yourself

Looking at plastics

1 Collect some small pieces of plastic.

2 How hard or soft are your pieces of plastic? Is it easy or difficult to scratch them with a metal nail? (BE CAREFUL!)

3 Put your pieces of plastic in a bowl of water, one at a time. Which of the pieces float? Which of them sink?

4 Try to bend your pieces of plastic. Which bend easily? Which are hard to bend?

5 Which pieces of plastic can you see through?

Glossary

chemical One of the thousands of substances which make up all living things and the world around them.

conservatory A room with glass walls and roof.

copper A reddish-brown metal used for pipes, wires, coins and some roofs.

dye A substance used to colour other material.

electrician A person who works with electricity.

fibre A very thin thread.

helmet A strong covering to protect your head.

lead A soft, heavy, grey metal.

manufacture To make something with machines.

material Any substance from which things are made.

melt To make something into a liquid by heating it.

mould A container for making things that will set in the shape that is wanted.

plastic A strong, light substance that can be made into many different shapes.

polystyrene A soft kind of plastic used for packing or to keep things warm or cool.

polythene A light plastic used to make bags and wrappings.

protect To keep safe.

recycle To treat waste material so that it can be used again.

rot To go soft or bad so that the object is useless.

rust The red or brown substance that forms on iron or steel in damp air.

waterproof Something that keeps water out is said to be waterproof.

Index

DUDLEY SCHOOLS LIBRARY
AND INFORMATION SERVICE

Schools Library and Information Services

S00000664956

DUDLEY SCHOOLS LIBRARY
AND INFORMATION SERVICE

Action for the Environment

Rubbish Disposal

Deborah Jackson Bedford

FRANKLIN WATTS
LONDON • SYDNEY

DUDLEY PUBLIC LIBRARIES

L 47489

664956   SCH

J628.4

© 2004 Franklin Watts

Franklin Watts
96 Leonard Street
London EC2A 4XD

Franklin Watts Australia
45–51 Huntley Street
Alexandria
NSW 2015

ISBN: 0 7496 5534 8

A CIP catalogue record for this book is
available from the British Library

Printed in Malaysia

Editor: Adrian Cole
Design: Proof Books
Art Director: Jonathan Hair
Picture Research: Kathy Lockley

Acknowledgements

Alice Springs Town Council: title page, 17 b. Courtesy of Apple: 13.
Martin Bond/Science Photo Library: 10 b. Leland Bobbe/© CORBIS:
29. Courtesy of The Body Shop: 27 b. Canterbury City Council, New
South Wales: 18 t, 19 b. Nick Cobbing/Still Pictures: 23 t.
DAS Fotoarchiv/Still Pictures: 17 t . © Digital Vision Ltd. All rights
reserved: 10 t, 20. © ENCAMS 8 b. Sarah Errington/
Eye Ubiquitous/Hutchison 5 t. Julio Etchart/Still Pictures: 8 t.
© Franklin Watts 9 t, 21 b, 22 t, 25 b, 25 t, 31. © Franklin
Watts/Chris Honeywell 4 b, 18 b. Dirk Frans/
Eye Ubiquitous/Hutchison: 5 b. Dylan Garcia/Still Pictures: Cover tl
Greenpeace/Cohen: 15 b. © GRRN: 23 b. Bruce Harber/Ecoscene:
27 t. Robert Harding Picture Library: 15 t. Crispin Hughes/
Eye Ubiquitous/Hutchison: 21 t. Martin Jones/Ecoscene: 11 t.
Keep Sweden Tidy Foundation: 9 b. Kevin King/Ecoscene: 19 t.
Maximilian Stock Ltd/Science Photo Library: 24. "PA" Photos /EPA:
11 b. Tony Page/Ecoscene: 28. Thomas Raupach/Still Pictures: 12 b.
Carlos Reyes-Manzo/Andes Press Agency: 2, 4 t, 6 t.
Peter Ryan/Science Photo Library: 22 b. Erik Schaffer/Ecoscene: 6 b.
Juergen Schmidt/ Still Pictures: 26. Hartmut Schwarzbach/Still
Pictures: 14. © 2003 Topham/Sean Sprague/Image World 7 b.

Contents

A load of rubbish!

Every day we dispose of things that we do not want any more, from food wrappers and vegetable scraps to old mobile phones and televisions. Billions of tonnes of rubbish are produced worldwide each year, which pollutes the environment and wastes valuable resources.

MAKING A DIFFERENCE

People all over the world are taking action to improve the way they dispose of rubbish, or to avoid creating it in the first place. They are making a real difference by recycling, reusing and reducing their rubbish.

Do you ever think about what happens to the rubbish you throw away? Where does it go?

HELPING HAND

There are many successful schemes that help people dispose of rubbish. For example, since recycling collections began in the USA in 1970, the amount of rubbish recycled has grown from 6% to 28%. Recycling saves natural resources and reduces pollution. While there is still more work to be done, new technology and changes in environmental laws mean that waste disposal methods are continually being improved.

A refuse collector takes away a bag of recycled rubbish. Today, more and more people recycle rubbish.

4

Action stations

The passing of environmental laws has helped to reduce the impact of rubbish disposal in some countries. In Ireland, so many plastic carrier bags were being thrown away that the government decided that shoppers should pay a tax on each bag. This law encouraged people to stop using plastic bags or to reuse them, and has reduced the number of bags being thrown away by a massive 90%.

Plastic carrier bags have been completely banned in Bangladesh because so many were dumped into rivers and drains that they caused serious flooding. Instead, people are encouraged to use traditional cloth bags made from the jute plant.

People at a street market in Bangladesh store their goods in jute bags, while this man (left) is using jute bags to carry his goats!

What do we do with it all?

Most of our rubbish is put into plastic sacks or bins and collected by refuse lorries to be buried at landfill sites or burned in incinerators. However, people are beginning to use alternative methods of rubbish disposal.

ALTERNATIVE METHODS

If we reuse something, then it does not become rubbish (see pages 16–17). Some things that cannot be reused can be recycled and made into something new (see pages 18–19). Kitchen and garden waste can be broken down and turned into compost by micro-organisms (see pages 18–19).

In developing countries, rubbish is mainly made up of fruit and vegetable waste and ash from fires. People reuse any valuable materials, such as metals.

WORLDWIDE WASTE

The way rubbish is disposed of varies widely. The Netherlands composts 86% of all its fruit, vegetable and garden waste. Some countries, such as Denmark, dispose of most of their unrecyclable waste in incinerators, while other countries, such as Australia, dispose of most of their waste in landfill sites.

In Germany, people are encouraged to reduce rubbish and 45% of their waste is recycled.

Action stations

Most countries have a waste management plan to help them deal with their rubbish. For example, in Hong Kong (below) there is very little space for landfill sites, so their waste management plan aims to reduce the amount of waste that is buried in such sites. People are encouraged to produce less rubbish and to reuse or recycle. Remaining waste is reduced in volume by incineration before it is put into landfill sites.

	UNITED STATES		UNITED KINGDOM		SWITZERLAND	
	Mid-1990s	1999/2000	Mid-1990s	1999/2000	Mid-1990s	1999/2000
Recycling	15%	22%	4%	9%	22%	32%
Composting	2%	6%	1%	2%	7%	14%
Incineration	16%	15%	9%	8%	59%	48%
Landfill	67%	57%	86%	81%	12%	6%

This table shows three countries that are recycling and composting more and burying or burning less. More and more countries recognise the importance of recycling.

Clear it up

Rubbish that is dumped or dropped spoils our environment and can cause many different hazards if it is not disposed of properly.

HAZARDS
Some rubbish causes a health hazard by attracting rats and flies, which can spread disease. Litter, such as broken glass bottles, plastic bags and discarded fishing line, can harm people and wildlife.

AGAINST THE LAW
Introducing laws is one way to stop people dumping rubbish wherever they want. For example, European laws force manufacturers of electrical equipment to collect and repair or recycle computers that they have sold.

Litter can spoil beaches, and can be carried by the sea from one country to another.

TIDY UP!
Campaigns, such as 'Keep Britain Tidy' and the European and South African 'Blue Flag Award' for clean beaches, remind people to put their litter in a bin, or to take it home with them.

Campaigns use posters and logos like this one to encourage everyone to be responsible and dispose of their rubbish carefully.

8

Action stations

The Eco-Schools award scheme encourages children throughout Europe to tidy up their school environment. It shows them how to tackle the problem of litter themselves and to teach others to dispose of their rubbish responsibly.

Design a poster to encourage people to put their litter in a bin. Make it bright and eye-catching to help get the message across. Illustrate your poster with pictures from magazines.

This poster has been made using artwork and real rubbish found in the playground.

Schoolgirls in Sweden holding an environmental banner as part of their involvement in the Eco-Schools scheme.

Filling up the land

Most rubbish we produce is buried in huge holes in the ground called landfill sites. Rubbish is taken there straight from our bins, squashed to reduce its size and spread over the site.

THE PROBLEM SITES

Landfill sites are a cheap way of rubbish disposal, but they are not a sustainable solution because space for sites is running out. Many people also believe that toxic liquids from the rubbish can pollute the local groundwater, killing wildlife and damaging farmland. Landfill sites also create methane, which is a greenhouse gas.

A bulldozer spreads rubbish over a landfill site. Later on, the rubbish will be covered in soil to stop it blowing away and attracting pests.

PRODUCING ENERGY

Some companies are taking advantage of landfill methane gas by using it as an alternative source of power. Methane can be used to generate electricity, instead of burning non-renewable fossil fuels, which produce carbon dioxide. For example, the car manufacturer BMW has a factory in Spartanburg, USA, that uses methane from a nearby landfill site to produce electricity and heat water.

The BMW factory in Spartanburg, USA, uses landfill methane gas to produce electricity and hot water.

LIFE AFTER LANDFILL

When landfill sites are full they cannot take any more waste. They are sealed with a covering of clay and soil and some can be landscaped and turned into public areas, such as golf courses, parks or even dry ski slopes. All landfill sites have to be closely monitored to ensure they do not begin to leak and pollute the surrounding land and water.

A recovered landfill site in Hong Kong. Such sites can become attractive places, but need careful looking after.

Action stations

At a meeting in Kyoto, Japan, in 1997, many countries agreed to reduce emissions of the greenhouse gases, including methane and carbon dioxide. These gases trap heat in the atmosphere and are believed to be making the Earth warmer. One way to reduce emissions is by recycling and composting more rubbish, which will cut the amount of greenhouse gases emitted by landfill sites and incinerators.

Campaigners at the Kyoto meeting hold up a globe made of silk.

Hazardous waste

Hazardous waste that is not disposed of properly is a threat to our health and the environment. Hazardous waste contains substances that are often explosive, toxic or highly flammable. It is mainly produced by factories and farms.

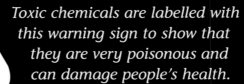

Toxic chemicals are labelled with this warning sign to show that they are very poisonous and can damage people's health.

MANAGING HAZARDOUS WASTE

New environmental laws require most hazardous waste to be pre-treated, which makes it safer, before it is buried in specially designed landfill sites. The most common way to dispose of hazardous liquid wastes, like oils and laboratory chemicals, is to incinerate them. However, many environmental groups, such as Greenpeace (see page 15), believe that both landfill sites and incineration can create serious health and environmental problems.

An engineer removes harmful chemicals from an old fridge before disposing of it.

WASTE REDUCTION

The best way to manage hazardous waste is to reduce the amount produced in the first place by:

• Using alternative nonhazardous materials, for example using environmentally-friendly cleaning products.

• Reducing the number of hazardous parts, for example using natural gas to cool fridges and freezers.

• Reusing items such as rechargeable batteries.

• Recovering and recycling materials, for example the silver used in photographic chemicals.

Action stations

Apple Computers is one example of a company that designs its products to have as little effect on the environment as possible. Their computers are energy-efficient, which means they use the minimum amount of power, and rely on lithium batteries, which are less hazardous for the environment. Apple work with a recycling company to recycle their old computers. This recycling can prevent as much as 90% of each computer ending up in a landfill site.

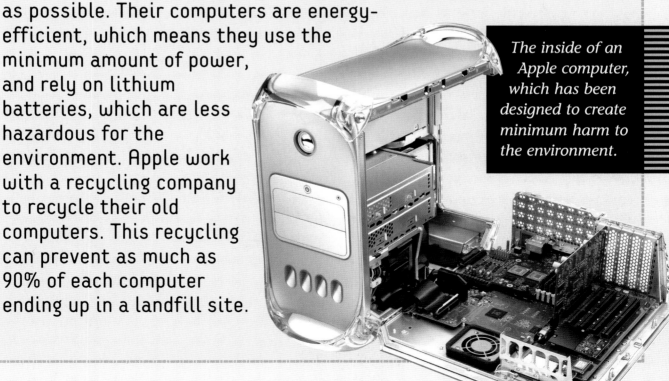

The inside of an Apple computer, which has been designed to create minimum harm to the environment.

Burning issues

Some rubbish is burned in huge furnaces called incinerators. Only a small amount of ash is left behind, which is usually buried in landfill sites.

INCINERATOR PROBLEMS

The smoke and ash from incinerators contain poisonous chemical pollutants which can harm people's health. Burning rubbish destroys resources that could be reused or recycled. Many organizations believe that incinerators cause more problems than they solve (see panel).

This incinerator in Germany converts the energy from burning rubbish into electricity.

BENEFITS OF BURNING

Burning rubbish means less waste is buried in landfill sites. Incinerators also have the advantage of producing electricity or hot water for powering and heating buildings. One kilogram of waste can power a light bulb for 10 hours. This saves using non-renewable fossil fuels, such as coal and gas.

The Green Heat scheme in Sheffield, UK, uses hot water produced by incinerating rubbish to heat buildings in the city.

Action stations

Greenpeace is campaigning to stop the incineration of rubbish. It recommends that people should sort their rubbish for composting or recycling before it is collected. Remaining waste could be processed by a new technology called Mechanical Biological Treatment to remove other valuable recyclable materials, before finally being reduced in special composters to make it safe for landfill.

Greenpeace campaigners protest outside an incinerator.

STOP INCINERATION

GREENPEACE

Reusable rubbish

The amount of rubbish we create is one of the greatest threats to our environment. But not everything we throw away is rubbish. Some things, such as old clothes or even faulty electrical goods, can be used for new purposes, or restored and given to people who need them.

Look what is in an average bin. Most of this rubbish could have been reused, recycled or composted instead of being thrown away.

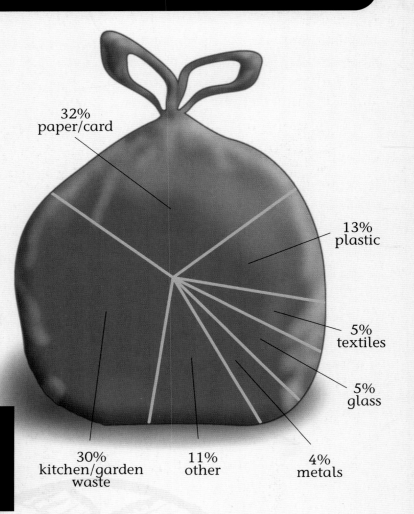

32% paper/card

13% plastic

5% textiles

5% glass

4% metals

11% other

30% kitchen/garden waste

A NEW PURPOSE

Reusing rubbish is an effective way of reducing the amount we throw away. Empty food containers, such as ice-cream tubs, can be reused for storing all kinds of things. Sometimes rubbish can be reused in a new way, like using old CDs for drinks mats or using old bottles and packages in sculptures.

AS GOOD AS NEW

If you cannot reuse something, it may be of use to someone else. Unwanted electrical items, for example washing machines, cookers and refrigerators, can be donated to special community-run schemes that clean and check them. The unwanted items are then given to people who cannot afford to buy new ones.

PRECIOUS RUBBISH

Because many people in developing countries are very poor and cannot afford to waste things, they reuse a lot of their rubbish. Materials such as old rubber car tyres are made into sandals, and aluminium cans are flattened and used as a cheap roofing for some houses.

A boy from Sudan in Africa holding a toy car he has made from reusable rubbish.

Action stations

Unwanted goods can often be sold to raise money. Many charities collect used items like mobile phones and postage stamps, which they sell to raise money to help others.

The Bowerbird Tip shop in Alice Springs, Australia, sells unwanted items like furniture, toys, bikes and building materials that people donate to the shop instead of throwing them away in the nearby landfill site.

Buying things from the tip shop helps to save valuable resources.

Bowerbird

What can we recycle?

Rubbish cannot always be reused, but this does not mean it has to be disposed of in a landfill site or an incinerator. Rubbish can also be recycled (made into something new). Glass, paper, metal, textiles, plastics and kitchen and garden waste can all be recycled.

RECYCLING

WHY DO WE NEED TO RECYCLE?

Many countries are adopting nationwide recycling schemes. The aim is to lower pollution levels by reducing the use of fossil fuels. The schemes mean that less rubbish has to be burnt or buried, which further reduces environmental damage. Making things from recycled materials uses less energy, saves valuable non-renewable resources such as oil and metal ores, and protects natural habitats and wildlife.

These workers separate the different sorts of rubbish on the conveyor belt before recycling.

READY FOR COMPOSTING

In some countries, vegetable, fruit and garden waste is collected separately from other rubbish and recycled into compost. Compost is made when worms, slugs and micro-organisms feed on this organic waste and break it down into a soil-like substance. The Netherlands has 24 special composting plants that recycle 1.5 million tonnes of waste a year into a rich fertilizer that is added back into the soil.

If your local authority does not collect waste for composting, why not have your own compost heap at school?

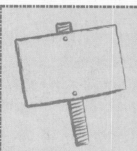

Action stations

The Living With Less Waste campaign in Canterbury City, Australia, makes recycling easy. Each home has a 'wheelie' bin to collect paper, card, glass, aluminium cans and plastic bottles. The bin is emptied every two weeks and the rubbish is taken away for recycling.

The Living With Less Waste campaign encourages people to recycle the items in this poster.

WHAT YOU CAN RECYCLE

PAPER AND CARDBOARD

NEWSPAPERS AND MAGAZINES

PLASTICS MARKED WITH ① ② ③ ④ ⑥

GLASS JARS AND BOTTLES

ALUMINIUM AND STEEL CANS, AEROSOLS

MILK AND JUICE CARTONS

PUT IT IN THE RIGHT BIN. WASTE HOTLINE 1300 791 222

LIVING WITH LESS WASTE

CANTERBURY CITY COUNCIL
City of Cultural Diversity

Paper for paper

Millions of trees are cut down every year to provide the raw material for making paper. In some countries, such as Indonesia, large areas of rainforest are being logged (cut down) for paper-making.

LOGGING

Logging destroys woodland habitats that are rich in different species of trees, plants and animals. Many trees are now specially grown on plantations, which replace old natural forests. Recycling paper also helps to protect these natural habitats.

Trees are cut down to provide the raw material for making paper.

PAPER-MAKING

Paper is made from plant fibres that are squashed, matted and dried. The raw material for paper is usually wood, but other natural resources such as cotton and straw can also be used. Every time we recycle paper we help to conserve these natural resources.

RECYCLING PAPER

Newspapers, telephone directories, magazines and computer paper can all be recycled. Waste paper is sorted and graded (separated into different types) before being mixed with water to make pulp. The pulp is cleaned and pressed into new paper. Paper can only be recycled about five times before the fibres become too weak. Recycling one tonne of paper saves about seventeen trees.

This woman in Malawi, Africa, works on a project that produces recycled paper.

Action stations

Look at some paper-packaged products, such as breakfast cereals, biscuits, chocolates, toothpaste, tissues and frozen foods. Check carefully on the packaging to see if it is made from recycled paper or card.

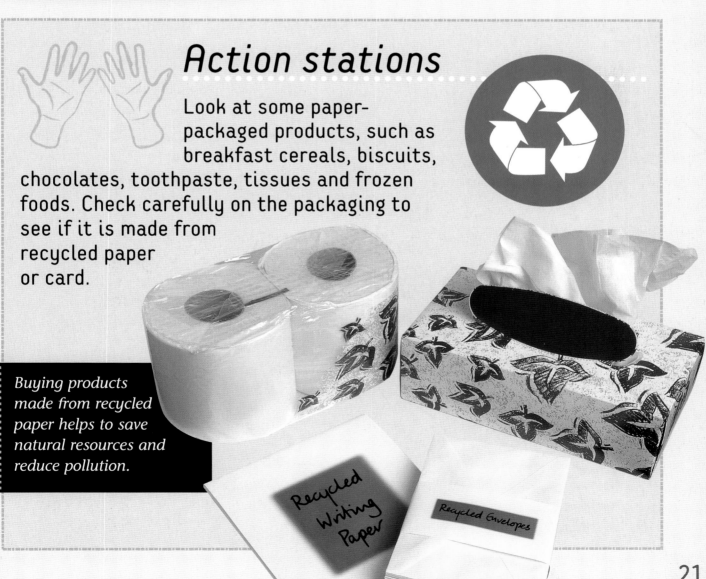

Buying products made from recycled paper helps to save natural resources and reduce pollution.

Recycled Writing Paper

Recycled Envelopes

Plastic problems

About 100 million tonnes of plastic are made from oil each year. Unfortunately, most plastics do not break down easily when they are thrown away. By recycling plastics we can help to reduce pollution and save landfill space and non-renewable resources.

GETTING SORTED

Recycling plastic is difficult because there are so many different types, such as polythene and PVC, that have to be reprocessed differently. These plastics must be sorted out before they can be recycled. But it is worth the effort: nearly two tonnes of oil are saved each time a tonne of polythene is recycled.

PLASTIC TECHNOLOGY

New processes can automatically identify and sort different types of plastic for recycling. For example, a technique called spectroscopy uses light to identify different plastics. This technology is used to sort the recyclable plastics in Melbourne, Australia.

Plastic bottles being inspected before recycling. The red rolls on the ground are made from similar recycled bottles.

RECYCLED PLASTIC

Recycled plastic is used in many things, including fleece jackets, furniture, seed trays, sewer pipes, video cases, carpets and the filling for sleeping bags.

This multi-coloured shop counter is made from Tectan, a board manufactured by pressing plastic bottles together.

Action stations

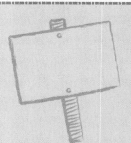

A campaign by the Grass Roots Recycling Network (GRRN) in the USA is encouraging manufacturers, including Pepsi and Coca-Cola, to reduce the effect that their products have on the environment. By using recycled plastic in the bottles they produce they could help save energy and resources, and reduce pollution and rubbish. Coca-Cola already use some recycled plastic in the bottles they sell in Europe, Australia and New Zealand.

The launch of the GRRN campaign to encourage Pepsi and Coca-Cola to reduce rubbish by reusing or recycling their bottles.

Metal and glass

Glass bottles and steel or aluminium cans are valuable because it takes a lot of energy to produce them. Recycling prevents this energy being wasted.

At this aluminium furnace, large amounts of energy are saved because recycled metal melts at a lower temperature than the raw materials that are used to produce it.

MAKING METAL

Recyclable metals are collected from recycling banks or extracted from household rubbish by strong magnets. Steel and aluminium are melted down in furnaces. The molten metal is then rolled into sheets and used to make products such as new cans, paper clips and even bicycles. Recycling aluminium uses just 5% of the energy needed to make aluminium from raw materials. Aluminium and steel can be recycled over and over again.

NEW GLASS FROM OLD

Glass for recycling is separated into different colours by using clear, green and brown 'bottle banks'. The sorted glass is cleaned before it is crushed into small pieces and melted in a furnace with other raw materials. The molten glass is then made into new bottles and jars. Recycling glass saves raw materials, such as sand, from being quarried and so helps to protect our environment.

Glass needs to be separated by colour before it is recycled.

Action stations

Look for the recycling symbols that are often printed on steel or aluminium cans (right). They show which metal the can is made from, helping us sort them for recycling. If there is no symbol, try pressing a magnet to the can. If it sticks, it is made of steel; if it does not, it is aluminium. Aluminium cans are easy to recognise by their shiny base and light weight.

RECYCLABLE STEEL

alu

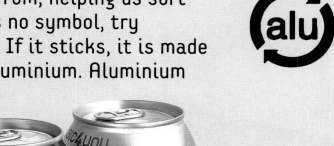

Magnets stick to steel cans, but not cans made from aluminium.

Cut down on rubbish

Many of the goods we buy are packaged. The packaging keeps things fresh and undamaged. Sometimes it also gives us important information about what we are buying. But discarded packaging which has only been used once makes up over 30% of the rubbish in our bins.

CHANGING OUR WAYS

By changing our shopping habits and buying products that are packaged simply, we will encourage more manufacturers to change the way they package their goods.

Shoppers in a Japanese supermarket. Many of the products in this picture have lots of packaging to make them look attractive.

RUBBISH REDUCTION

Some manufacturers are already reducing the amount or weight of packaging they use. Others are making packaging from biodegradable or recycled materials. We can easily reduce the amount of packaging we throw away by being careful about what we buy. When we go shopping we should:

• Buy concentrated, refillable products, such as soap powder.

• Avoid over-packaged or individually-wrapped goods.

• Choose products wrapped in recyclable packaging.

• Buy products made from recycled materials.

• Reuse plastic bags or use a rucksack to carry shopping.

A bottle deposit and return machine in Denmark. This encourages people to bring back empty bottles for reuse or recycling.

Action stations

Some companies package their products in a way that has the least impact on the environment. A company called the Body Shop uses the minimum amount of packaging for its products, and recycles empty packaging returned by its customers. By using recycled plastic in its bottles — such as the one on the right — it saves the equivalent of about 4 million new bottles every year.

Buying rubbish

Remembering the 3 Rs – Reduce, Reuse and Recycle – will help us solve the problem of rubbish. We need to reduce the amount we buy and throw away, reuse as many things as possible, and recycle anything else we can.

BUYING LESS

Everything we buy will eventually end up as rubbish. Instead of reusing and mending the things we already have, we often throw them away and buy new ones instead. Buying less and recycling or reusing more would reduce rubbish and save resources, energy and money.

Broken fridges are often thrown away because it can be more expensive to repair them than to buy a new one.

WHO MAKES THE MOST RUBBISH?

Developed countries, such as the UK and USA, throw away much more rubbish than developing countries, such as Bangladesh and Nigeria. In developing countries people are often too poor to buy many new things and so reuse as much as they can.

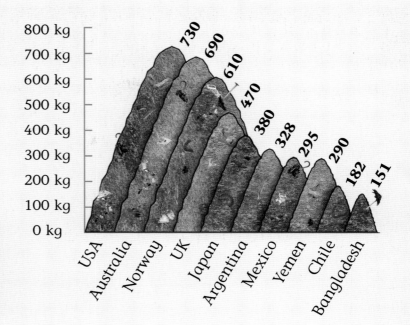

This graph shows the average amount of rubbish thrown out by each person in various countries in the year 2000.

Action stations

People often buy things they do not really need. Have you ever bought something and then only used it once or twice?

Before you buy something, ask yourself:
- What is it made from?
- Are any of the materials recycled?
- Is the packaging really necessary?
- Do I really need it?
- If I buy it – do I need a carrier bag?

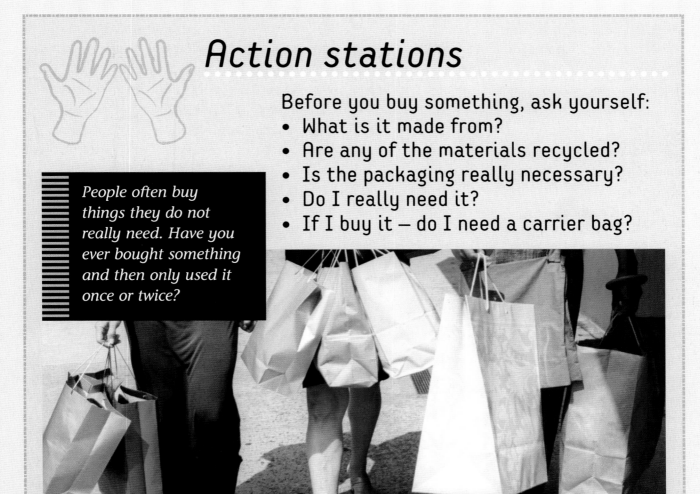

Glossary

Biodegradable When a material can be broken down and decayed by bacteria and other micro-organisms.

Campaigns Action taken by people or groups, such as Greenpeace, to try to persuade others to change what they do.

Compost A soil-like mixture, made from decaying fruit, vegetables and plants.

Deposit and return system A system in which customers pay an extra charge when they buy bottles of soft drink or beer. They reclaim this money when they return the empty bottles.

Developed countries Wealthier countries with very developed industries.

Developing countries Poorer countries, which rely more on farming than on industry.

Emissions Waste gases, such as methane and carbon dioxide, which are discharged into the air from chimneys or landfill sites.

Environmental laws Laws that help to protect the environment.

Flammable A material that catches fire very easily.

Fossil fuels Fuels such as oil, natural gas or coal that have formed over millions of years from the remains of plants and animals.

Greenhouse gases Gases such as methane and carbon dioxide which are produced from decaying rubbish or burning fossil fuels. These gases trap heat in the atmosphere and are causing a gradual rise in the Earth's temperature.

Habitat The environment where plants and animals live, such as a river, meadow or jungle.

Incinerate To burn something in an incinerator and reduce it to ashes.

Local authority The local council who are in charge of running services, like rubbish disposal, in an area.

Micro-organisms Very small living things, such as bacteria, that can only be seen with a microscope.

Natural resources Raw materials that are taken from the environment, such as sand, water and oil. Some natural resources, such as wood, can be replaced by replanting.

Non-renewable resources Resources such as coal, oil, gas and metal ores which have taken millions of years to form. These resources cannot be replaced.

Packaging The containers that products come in, such as cans, boxes or plastic bags.

Pollution Harmful gases, chemicals or rubbish which have been released into the environment.

Tax Money that has to be paid to the government when something is bought or used.

Textiles Woven fabrics that are used in items such as clothes and bags.

Toxic Very poisonous. Toxic waste can harm people, wildlife and the environment.

Waste management plan A set of decisions taken by a local area or a country to help it dispose of its waste.

Find out more

**www.defra.gov.uk/environment/
waste/index.htm**
Look on this site for information about
rubbish reduction, reuse, recycling
and other rubbish disposal topics.

www.cashforcans.co.uk
Click on this site for an interactive tour
of a recycling plant and discover what
happens when cans are recycled.

www.eco-schools.org.uk
Discover how to tackle the problem of
litter in your school.

www.greenpeace.org
Find out about Greenpeace's campaigns
concerning rubbish disposal. Links to all
the national Greenpeace groups.

www.hdra.org.uk
Visit this site to find out how to make a
compost heap for recycling kitchen and
garden waste.

**www.ollierecycles.com/aus
www.ollierecycles.com/uk**
A fun site designed for children to promote
the 3 Rs – reduce, recyle, reuse – with
ideas for projects and puzzles and games.

www.wasteonline.org.uk
This site is packed with information about
the different types of rubbish we produce.

www.zerowaste.co.nz
This site is dedicated to working towards
zero waste. It has links to similar projects
in New Zealand, Australia and the UK.

31

Index